PENNSY

Published by Gallery Books
A Division of W H Smith Publishers Inc.
112 Madison Avenue
New York, New York 10016

Produced by
Brompton Books Corp.
15 Sherwood Place
Greenwich, CT 06830

ISBN 0-8317-6806-1

Printed in Hong Kong

10 9 8 7 6 5 4 3 2 1

LVANIA

TEXT   BARBARA ANGLE HABER

DESIGN   ADRIAN HODGKINS

GALLERY BOOKS
An imprint of W.H. Smith Publishers Inc.
112 Madison Avenue
New York, New York 10016

To Walt, Jill, and Holly

PHOTO CREDITS

Martin Armstrong: 20.
I. George Bilyk: 1, 19, 27, 30, 32, 33, 40, 50-51.
Malcolm Emmons: 99.
Phil Kramer: 3-6, 16-17, 28, 29, 38, 39, 41, 44.
Paul Pavlik: 95, 126-127.
Chuck Place: 56-57, 58, 59.
Ponzini Photgraphy: 31.
Blair Seitz, Seitz and Seitz, Inc., Harrisburg, PA: 18, 21, 22-23, 24,
    25, 26, 34-35, 36, 37, 42, 43, 45, 47, 48-49, 52, 53, 54, 55,   60,
61, 62-63, 65, 66-67, 68-69, 70, 71, 72-73, 74-75, 76, 77, 78,   79,
80, 81, 82-83, 85, 86, 87, 88-89, 91, 92-93, 94, 96, 97, 98,   100-101,
102, 103, 104, 105, 106, 107, 108-109, 116, 120, 121, 124,   128.
Hank Somma: 117, 119, 123.
Andrew Wagner: 111, 112-113, 114-115, 118, 125.

1 *"We The People": A brass band in colonial garb
marches in Philadelphia's celebration of the 200th
anniversary of the signing of the Constitution.*

3/6 The Philadelphia skyline.

INTRODUCTION

When William Penn sailed aboard the *Welcome* up the Delaware River in 1682, virtually 90 percent of his new province was forested. White pine and hemlock thickened the northern hills while chestnut, oak, black walnut, hickory, and maple spread throughout the southern portion. Today Penn's Woods still cover 60 percent of the state. Unbroken stretches of forest, broad rivers, racing streams, and lush farmland combine to provide as inviting a panorama to the modern traveler as they did when Penn first beheld the land that would flourish under his "holy experiment."

Penn was disappointed by the English Privy Council's rejection of his name for the colony, New Wales. His alternative proposal—Silvania, meaning woodlands—was acceptable. King Charles II added the surname Penn to honor William's father, Admiral William Penn, and signed the charter on March 4, 1681. William Penn became governor of 28,000,000 acres across the sea, land he had not yet even seen.

Penn converted to the Quaker faith as a young man and was eager to formulate a system of government in a new land. Although it took over a year before he was able to set foot in his province, he devoted that time to zealous promotion. Seeking to "give the liberties we ask," he arrived on October 27, 1682 with his Frame of Government, extending to its citizenry absolute freedom of worship, personal and property rights, and the privilege of self-government.

Penn inherited a European population of about 500, a reflection of colonization that passed from Swedish to Dutch and finally to English control. As a direct result of Penn's pamphlets, immigration increased the population to 20,000 by the year 1700. English settled in the eastern portion, Germans in the central limestone valleys with rich, loamy soil, and Scotch-Irish in the rugged mountains of western Pennsylvania.

The greater population was, of course, native American. For centuries these peoples had lived here, and for decades they had dealt with white men in vigorous fur trade. Influenced by Quaker philosophy, Penn sent a remarkable letter addressed to "My Friends" advising the Indians of his "resolution to live justly, peaceably and friendly with you." His fair dealing with the native Americans assured friendly relations for 50 years.

In August 1684 boundary disputes with Maryland forced Penn to return to England to ensure that Philadelphia, the city he planned, remained in Pennsylvania. His second visit to the province lasted from November 1699 until the fall of 1701. During this period he refined his definition of representative government into the famous Charter of Privileges. But once again Penn hastened to London, this time to prevent William and Mary from bringing Pennsylvania under the rule of the crown. In 1712 a stroke rendered him incapable of returning to his proprietorship. William Penn died in 1718. Although his sojourns were barely three years total, Penn's imprint on his woodland colony was indelible.

Colonial Pennsylvania prospered and expanded westward. In October 1753, George Washington, a major at the tender age of 21, volunteered to deliver a message from British authorities at Williamsburg, Virginia, to the French of Fort Le Boeuf (present-day Waterford) politely requesting their departure. The reply that Washington brought back was a refusal to comply with British demands.

In May 1754 Colonel Washington returned to southwestern Pennsylvania to construct a stockade he called Fort Necessity, which he then almost immediately surrendered to the French. A year later the French and Indians won a decisive battle at Fort Duquesne at the forks of the Allegheny and Monongahela rivers. There they crushed the British army commanded by valiant General Edward Braddock, who fell mortally wounded.

Pennsylvania's amicable relations with the Indians gradually crumbled as time eroded Penn's impact on the new colony. The native friends grew discontent after the "Walking Purchase" in 1737 when Penn's sons John, Thomas, and Richard deceived them by hiring runners to stake out the claim a man could "walk" in a day and a half. Furthermore, the native Americans fundamentally believed that the land and its bounty were to be shared, as one shares the skies above, not surrendered.

In the spring of 1763, Chief Pontiac of the Ottowas created an alliance of tribes from Ohio, Pennsylvania, and the Great Lakes. In coordinated surprise attacks, they captured nine British forts in western Pennsylvania and Ohio. Their purpose was to reclaim lands occupied by English settlers on both sides of the Alleghenies. On August 5, Pontiac's War culminated in the bloody battle at Bushy Run about 20 miles from Fort Pitt (formerly Fort Duquesne), where Colonial Henry Bouquet wrought victory from near defeat. White men's raids and Indian revenge sullied the record of "living friendly together" espoused by the Quakers.

In the east, Philadelphia was growing. So named by its founder because it literally means "brotherly love" in Greek, Philadelphia was designed to be a "greene Country Towne." By the middle of the eighteenth century, the country town was a city spreading on the banks of the Delaware and Schuylkill rivers. Its harbor was large enough to accommodate schooners, and brisk international trade ensued in its busy port, where pig iron and bar iron produced in Pennsylvania were exported.

The First Continental Congress convened in Carpenters' Hall in 1774 to address colonial grievances. Philadelphia's central location and its prominence in colonial affairs made it a natural selection. In the old State House, the best minds in the 13 colonies hammered out the resounding Declaration of Independence in 1776. Penn's "seed of a nation" took root and flowered again in 1787 when the Constitutional Convention replaced the Articles of Confederation with a new Constitution proposing a strong federal government. Philadelphia, seat of the Congress from 1790 to 1800, became the birthplace of the nation and its first permanent capital.

Meanwhile, small inland cities such as Lancaster, York, and Reading were thriving local centers for German farmers, glassmakers like "Baron" Henry William Stiegel of Manheim, and ironmasters such as Peter Grubb of Cornwall. Carpenters and wheelwrights were manufacturing unique Conestoga wagons near Lancaster. So steady was commerce between Lancaster and Philadelphia that a turnpike joining the cities was built in

1794. Using the ideas of a Scotch engineer, John Loudon McAdam, this first "macadam" road in America was designed to bear the heavy weight of the rumbling Conestoga wagons.

As development stretched westward, a system of canals linking east and west spread across the state. The era of canals, roughly 1820 to 1880, contributed significantly to westward expansion, but was relatively short-lived because of difficulties in maintaining the canals. They were ultimately replaced by railroads.

Iron made the colonies independent. Eastern Pennsylvania had equipped the revolutionary soldiers, but by the Civil War the center of the iron industry was Pittsburgh, where the heavy ordnance was produced for Union forces. Pennsylvania's 97 billion tons of coal comprised the nation's majority of bituminous (soft) coal and all of its anthracite (hard) coal. Timber, essential to the iron and steel industries, was abundant.

Edwin L. Drake's successful drilling for oil at Titusville in 1859 created almost as much frenzy as the California gold rush had a decade earlier. The romance of the oil boom and bust was enacted in the remote hills of western Pennsylvania. Production escalated until near the turn of the century, when black gold was discovered in Texas and the surge went west.

The only Pennsylvanian to become President of the United States, James Buchanan, believed that through compromise he could preserve the Union in 1856. "Old Buck" waged a victorious "front porch campaign" from Wheatland, his home in Lancaster, but he endured a sorely troubled presidency. Factionalism and secession propelled the country into chaos, resulting in the Civil War.

In the summer of 1863 Gettysburg was a very small town of only 2000. On its golden wheatfields, in its orchards and among its rounded hills raged a three-day battle, from July 1-3, that reversed the tide of the Civil War and determined the fate of the nation. On November 19, 1863, war-weary President Abraham Lincoln arrived to dedicate a national cemetery to the 7058 men who died there. His moving Gettysburg Address remains one of the most famous speeches in history.

The Civil War changed the country's economy from primarily agrarian to industrial. Towns sprinkled throughout Pennsylvania built factories to manufacture shoes, mills to weave textiles, and foundries to produce iron and steel. Pittsburgh best represents this intense industrial concentration. Located near then newly-probed iron mines near Lake Superior and almost directly atop major sources of bituminous coal, Pittsburgh attracted astute business titans such as Andrew Carnegie, Henry Clay Frick, and Andrew Mellon.

Early steelmaking was devoted to producing rails for westward expansion. By the turn of the century, steel was being produced for building, tin cans were introduced, and wire was manufactured for the rapidly growing network of telephone and telegraph systems. After the accelerated production required during World War II, many of these mills, mines, and factories were closed because of decline in demand or relocation to areas where cheaper labor reduced costs.

Nowhere is the supreme effort to correct urban industrial problems more striking than in Pittsburgh. Its "renaissance" borders on the miraculous. A city literally choking to death, where street lights burned at nine o'clock in the morning and citizens donned masks to protest suffocating smog, Pittsburgh began to come up for air in the late 1940s. It took years to eradicate slums, rip out decaying buildings and create the Golden Triangle, but by 1970 the major thrust was accomplished and the "Smoky City" had cleaned itself up.

Pennsylvania's place in history and its blend of mountains, tapestried fields, quaint towns, and urban attractions offer ideal opportunities for touring and recreation. Pennsylvanians welcome visitors warmly and trust that those who explore its delights will feel the same affection for the state as they do.

PHILADELPHIA

Philadelphia is a marvelous place to walk. Paramount on any visitor's list is Independence National Historical Park, "the most historic square mile in America." Centerpiece of a cluster of perfectly preserved eighteenth-century buildings is Independence Hall, just across from the Liberty Bell Pavilion. Carpenters' Hall and Congress Hall are also here. Visitors can slip into pews where George Washington, Benjamin Franklin, and Betsy Ross once worshipped in lovely old Christ Church, and then wander through its burial ground where lie the remains of Benjamin Franklin and other noted colonial and Revolutionary War figures. A modern steel skeleton outlines the framework of Franklin's home in Franklin's Court.

Not far from Independence Park is Penn's Landing, a promenade on the Delaware River. Tourists can literally stand in Commodore Dewey's footprints on the USS *Olympia* where he gave the order, "You may fire when you are ready, Gridley," in Manila Bay during the Spanish-American War. The guppy-class World War II submarine USS *Becuna* bobs a few feet away. Perhaps the handsome square-rigged *Gazela* of Philadelphia will also be in port.

If walking becomes tiring, it's fun to take a Victorian-type trolley bus on a tour of Fairmount Park's magnificent preserve on both sides of the Schuylkill River. Eight colonial mansions as well as Philadelphia's superb Museum of Art are located within the park. While joggers, cyclists, and horseback riders explore its shady paths, scullers leave Boathouse Row for an afternoon on the river. Facilities are provided for every major sport as well as bocce, cricket, rugby, and archery, and it's possible to picnic anywhere. America's first zoo includes a delightful Children's Petting Zoo. Just beyond Boathouse Row is Fairmount Waterworks, a Roman Revival temple that housed steam engines and water wheels for the city's water supply.

Among the 40 museums within the city limits are the Rodin Museum, the Franklin Institute Science Museum, the Mummers Museum, the Norman Rockwell Museum (featuring all his *Saturday Evening Post* covers), and the United States Mint.

Downtown shopping is a treat at landmark John Wanamaker, where one can relax at daily concerts given on a magnificent pipe organ. Tempting boutiques now occupy a newly-renovated Victorian Merchants' Exchange, the Bourse, just opposite Liberty Bell Pavilion. A Philadelphia institution, elegant Strawbridge and Clothier, is located in the smashing new Gallery. Designer apparel for men and women is famed Nan Duskin's attraction.

No visit to the Philadelphia area would be complete without a stroll through exquisite Longwood Gardens in any season. Its conservatory and greenhouses cover three and a half glass-enclosed acres. The outdoor gardens are renowned for the spectacular Festival of Fountains, choreographed to music and light. About 25 miles southwest of the city at Chadd's Ford, in an imaginatively converted stone grist mill on an unspoiled riverbank, the Brandywine River Museum exhibits works of three generations of Wyeths.

About 25 miles west of Philadelphia, costumed interpreters recreate the atmosphere of the six-month encampment of Washington's beleaguered troops during the harsh winter of 1777-78 at Valley Forge. Washington's headquarters and reconstructed soldiers' huts on original redoubts and fortifications make a fascinating self-guided tour.

15 Once the old State House for the Province of Pennsylvania, Independence Hall symbolizes the adoption of the Declaration of Independence and the creation of the United States Constitution. America does start here.

16/17 Seen from the Museum of Art, Philadelphia's spires gleam in the morning sun. Washington Monument faces Benjamin Franklin Parkway and City Hall.

18 Atop City Hall, William Penn has the best view of what has become of his planned "greene Country Towne." The 37-foot-tall bronze statue stares out at early morning commerce on the Delaware River and Camden, New Jersey beyond.

19 Towering 945 feet, the shining Art Deco-style office building at One Liberty Place is the newest structure in downtown Philadelphia. Completed in 1987, it broke the unwritten law that no building shall rise higher than the height of William Penn on City Hall.

20 "Proclaim Liberty throughout all the land unto all the inhabitants thereof." The Liberty Bell rang out on July 8, 1776 and on the anniversary of Independence Day, July 4, until 1835. As it tolled for Chief Justice John Marshall on July 8, 1835, it cracked.

21 Since January 1, 1976, the Liberty Bell has resided in its own pavilion. Tentative fingers often stretch out to touch this beloved symbol of freedom.

24 Auguste Rodin's powerful study of profound contemplation, the bronze masterpiece "The Thinker," broods at the entrance to the Rodin Museum. The outstanding collection includes "The Burghers of Calais" and "The Gates of Hell."

22/23 Rudolf Siemering's heroic stone and bronze Washington Monument commands the base of the Philadelphia Museum of Art.

25 An Aegean-blue sky enhances this view of the south wing of the Philadelphia Museum of Art. Built on the model of a Greek temple, the exterior with its Ionic columns, colorful frieze and lively detail is itself a work of art.

26 Exploding with color in any season, the Longwood Gardens are renowned for elaborate fireworks and fountains choreographed to music throughout the summer.

27 The Clothesline Art Exhibit attracts serious study in Philadelphia's famed Rittenhouse Square.

28 Congress Hall was the meeting place of the United States Congress from its completion in 1790 until 1800. It is now a museum.

29 The first Continental Congress met at Carpenters' Hall on September 5, 1774. From 1791 to 1797 it was the home of the first United States Bank.

30 Superstar Mick Jagger of the Rolling
Stones performs at the Philadelphia Spectrum,
a major venue for big-name entertainers.

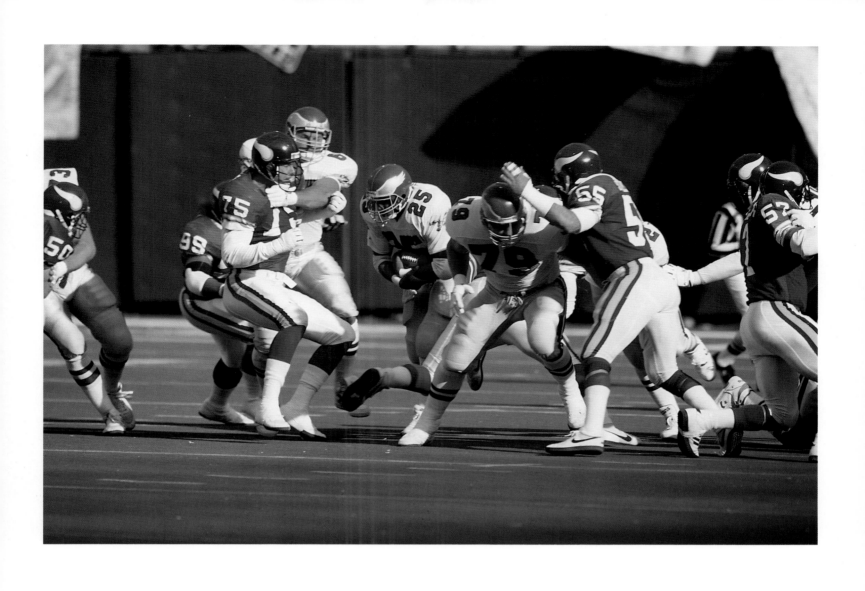

*31 Anthony Toney (25) of the Philadelphia
Eagles cradles the ball as he drives forward
on the astroturf at Veterans Stadium.*

32 Fore or aft, nothing compares to the fabulous Mummers. On New Year's Day in Philadelphia, stringbands play "Oh, Dem Golden Slippers" when female impersonators in elaborate costumes march down Broad Street.

33 Modern dancers seem to be saluting the wonders of the Franklin Institute Science Museum. Inside are computers, demonstrations, and a walk-through heart, on four floors of space devoted to science and technology.

34/35 Hugging the banks of the river, Boathouse Row, the base for the "Schuylkill
Navy," is transformed into a fantasyland after
dark.

36 The Gazela of Philadelphia rests at her
berth in Penn's Landing on the Delaware
River. The proud three-masted vessel has set
sail since her launching in Portugal in 1883.

37 Intent on docking, a sculler completes his effort on the Schuylkill River.

38 The newly-renovated Bourse now accommodates 50 shops and restaurants.

39 Elfreth's Alley, the oldest residential street in America, invites strollers to step back into the eighteenth century.

40 Up and away! Fourth of July festivities include balloon races over the city.

41 Dazzling Independence Day fireworks burst over the largest steel sailing ship in the world, the Moshulu, at Penn's Landing.

42 One of eight elegant mansions in Fairmount Park, Mount Pleasant was built in 1761 by a privateering Scottish sea captain, John Macpherson. Sadly, Peggy Shippen, bride of Benedict Arnold, never moved into the home he bought for her as a wedding gift.

43 The interior of Mount Pleasant reflects the gracious way of life in colonial Philadelphia.

44 On location at Valley Forge, actor Barry Bostwick convincingly portrays George Washington in a TV mini-series about the revolutionary commander.

45 Reenactments create an atmosphere of authenticity at Valley Forge Historic Park. Here a colonial general reviews his militia on French Alliance Day.

EASTERN PENNSYLVANIA

Forming the eastern boundary of Pennsylvania, the Delaware River resolutely cuts its way south, changing character on its long journey. Broad stretches afford excellent canoeing, spring-fed rapids challenge the adventurous, and gentle currents woo "tubers" to spin lazily downstream. After carving the scenic Delaware Water Gap's great gorge, the river tumbles along past industrial centers before flowing into Delaware Bay.

Some of the loveliest of Penn's Woodlands are in northeast Pennsylvania. If one could choose, late June is the time to experience Delaware State Forest, when miles of shell-pink and china-white mountain laurel dazzle the eye and scent the air. Summer beckons on Lake Wallenpaupack. Autumn in the Poconos braces the spirit. In these popular resorts, falling snow is not cause for delay but reason to frolic.

Interstate Route 81 bisects central Pennsylvania's coal region and links its primary centers: Scranton, Wilkes Barre, and Hazelton. An unheralded jewel of this alpine region is Carbon County seat Jim Thorpe. Faced with financial disaster as the area's lumber and mining ventures failed, this determined town changed its name from Mauch Chunk and altered its destiny. Now an engaging Victorian restoration, Jim Thorpe is a mecca for whitewater rafters, hang-gliders and visitors to Laurel Blossom and Fall Foliage festivals.

The Star of Bethlehem shines on South Mountain. On Christmas Eve 1741, Count Nicholas Ludwig von Zinzendorf heard cattle lowing nearby and named this German Moravian settlement Bethlehem. The Christmas City glorifies the holidays with colorful festivals of light and music. In May Bethlehem commemorates its Moravian heritage in a Musikfest of Bach performances, trombone choirs, candlelight, and vesper concerts. Festivity reigns in Bethlehem in every season.

Bucks County's signature is understated elegance. Gracing the shores of the rippling Delaware River or overlooking the still waters of the Delaware Canal are stately limestone homes set on manicured lawns. William Penn chose Bucks County for Pennsbury Manor, his handsome country home, which has been reconstructed near Morrisville. Ice cream fans as well as antique lovers flock to New Hope, an artists' colony on the Delaware. For those who would rather not ride an inner-tube or paddle down the river, a barge drawn by mules on a shaded towpath glides along the sleepy canal. In Washington Crossing Historic Park, Washington's bold strategy to capture Trenton is reenacted annually on Christmas Day.

Berks and Lebanon counties offer a pleasing symmetry of contoured fields balanced with small picturesque towns. Hopewell Furnace National Historic Site near Birdsboro is an outstanding restoration of an ironmaster's plantation. Founded in 1748 by William Penn's sons, Reading is a manufacturing and discount center that attracts many out-of-town shoppers. Lebanon annually celebrates the area's most famous product, tangy Lebanon bologna, in August. In the heart of Lebanon Valley, one can tour rustic wooden smokehouses where bologna is cold-smoked, Michter's Distillery where the "whiskey that warmed the Revolution" is still produced from sour mash, and sylvan Mount Gretna, unchanged and unspoiled after a hundred years.

47 Established by Peter Grubb in 1742, the Cornwall Iron Furnace in Lebanon County provided 42 cannon during the Revolutionary War, and the iron mine operated until 1974. This Gothic revival detail is from the well-preserved furnace building which was enlarged in 1857.

48/49 In southeastern Berks County, Hopewell Village is a living museum that reproduces the lifestyle on an iron plantation. In the foreground outside the casting house are piles of flasks, used in molding lighter and more detailed iron plates.

50/51 From a lookout on the Appalachian Trail, two "plain" girls survey Penn's Woods and a patchwork quilt of farmland.

52 Droplets of early morning dew wash the fragile blossoms of mountain laurel. The state flower, as fragrant as it is lovely, blooms extravagantly in the Poconos.

53 Buck Hill Falls thunders down in the Pocono Mountains, where spectacular waterfalls abound.

54 Like a child's scrawl, Bucks County
Playhouse is written on the waters. Here
Broadway productions are staged in a 200-
year-old converted mill.

55 Mule power hauls a barge along sleepy
Delaware Canal in New Hope, Bucks County.

56/57 Maples along a tiny stream blaze with
fall color in the Poconos.

58 A warm sun burnishes their coats as these horses graze at a small farm near Pipersville in Bucks County.

59 Surrounded by samples of his work, Ernst Newhart demonstrates early printing techniques at the Old Franklin Print Shop in New Hope.

60 Young and old catch railroad fever at Scranton's Steamtown U.S.A. Steam locomotives carry tourists on scenic excursions through the Poconos.

61 Constructed to replace a scar left by a stone quarry on the summit of Mount Penn in Reading, a pagoda similar to Nayoga Castle in Japan offers a splendid panorama of the city at sunset.

62/63 Aglow with Christmas wonder, Bethlehem celebrates its christening by Moravian missionaries on Christmas Eve in 1741.

LANCASTER COUNTY: DUTCH HEARTLAND

Pennsylvania! Spontaneous images bubble up: horse-drawn buggies clip-clopping down sleepy roads, quaint folk in plain clothing, shy rounded ladies in bonnets and white caps, markets where every vegetable seems to be polished, groaning boards laden with irresistible delicacies. Incredibly, this world still exists, and Lancaster County best illustrates it.

"Gentle people" were among the original settlers. William Penn's guaranteed right to follow one's conscience attracted sects whose strict practices included unadorned dress, worship in homes rather than churches, and refusal to swear allegiance to any authority.

Strictest of these groups are the disciples of Jacob Amman—the Amish, who shun twentieth-century mechanization and public schooling. Bearded men wear broad-brimmed black felt hats with frock coats and trousers fastened with hooks and eyes, buttons being "too worldly." Married women and girls wear solid colors only, favoring lavender and cornflower-blue dresses. Makeup is forbidden. Their hair, never cut, is parted in the center and worn in a bun, then covered with a white cap. Boys, their blond bangs peeping under broad hats, look like miniature adults. It is not unusual to see a patient horse tied to a post in a supermarket parking lot, while his driver selects items she cannot grow or stitch at home.

These people tend the land with special love. On some of the richest farmland in the world the Amish plow vast fields with teams of mules or horses. Amish, Mennonites, and Dunkards seek merely to follow their faith and pursue their customs.

Somehow the city of Lancaster retains a small-town feeling. The Red Rose City's Central Market, redolent with aromas of home-baked breads and cakes, presents a dazzling array of mouth-watering meats, cheeses, and produce. Appetizing discoveries abound: schmierkase (soft mellow cheese), pungent sauerkraut, pink hard-boiled eggs pickled in vinegar and red beet juice, "snitz und knepp" (dried apple slices and doughy dumplings cooked with ham), hot bacon dressing, golden chicken pot pies, and shoofly pie, a gooey confection of molasses and crumbs.

One doesn't have to go to market to find fresh produce. Roadside stands pop up with amazing frequency. Plump tomatoes, fat cucumbers, and piles of just-plucked corn are displayed with appropriate prices and a cigar box to put payment in.

Visitors should pause to listen to the distinctive Pennsylvania patois, a melodic undulating lilt usually ending on an up-note. Much exaggeration has been made of Pennsylvanians' literal German translation to English, like "Throw the cow over the fence some hay." Although at times a heavy Dutch pronunciation is audible, music and rhythm better characterize local speech patterns.

The best way to savor the delights of Lancaster County is to slacken one's pace to about the speed of a spirited horse as he steps lively on a rural road curling through cornfields. With good fortune the path may cross a covered bridge or cut through a farm where barefoot children romp after chores. Following Robert Frost's decision to take a road "less traveled by" will make "all the difference."

65 Creating a geometry in shades of green, Amish farmers near Lancaster cling to primitive methods with abundant results.

66/67 Laundry hangs out to dry at an Amish farmhouse. Busy as they are with chores and cooking, the women find time for tending gardens and growing flowers.

68/69 Skillfully handling his team of six mules, an Amish boy creates a cloud of dust as he harrows rich Lancaster County soil.

70 A lollipop is some consolation as this Amish youngster waits patiently for his parents.

71 Listening to the rhythm of the horse's hooves, an Amish farmer drives to market with baskets of ripe peaches.

72/73 The photographer has caught the attention of Amish children walking home from school. The boys seem to be curious, but the girls are shy because they know they are not supposed to be photographed.

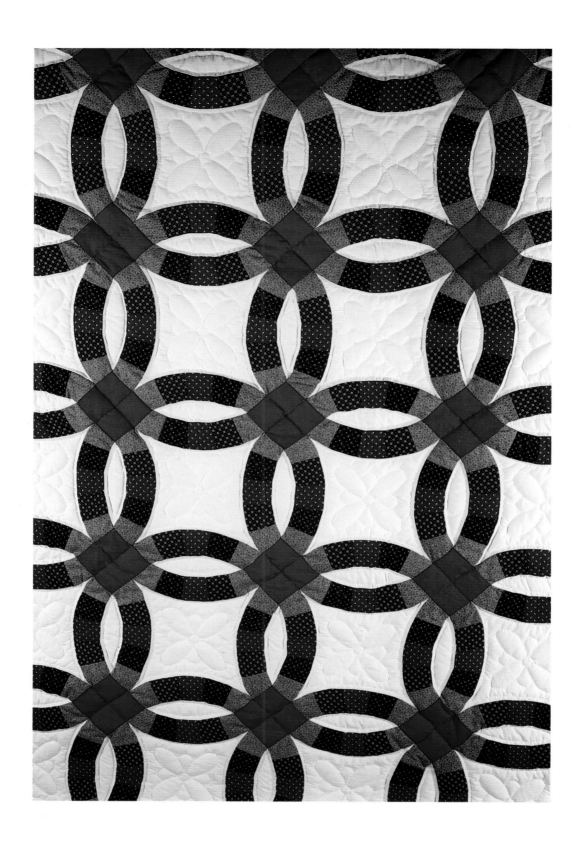

74/75 Buggies at rest outside an Amish home indicate Sunday morning worship. Observances such as weddings and funerals also take place in the homes. The Amish do not worship in a formal church.

76 Meticulously stitched, this fanciful Wedding Ring pattern was discovered at Naomi Fisher's Quilt Store in Bird-in-Hand.

77 This whimsical pattern is called "Trip Around the World."

78 Rural traffic passes by hex signs on a barn caught in a sunny spotlight.

79 Early morning light silhouettes workers perched on the ribs of a new structure during a barn-raising. With a philosophy of "one for all," these Old Order Mennonites devote one day's effort to a friend.

80 Lancaster's historic Central Market bursts with summer's plenty. Locally grown fruits and vegetables are plucked morning-fresh from the fields.

81 There's always a new twist at the Sturgis Pretzel Bakery in Lititz, where the ticket of admission is a pretzel. You can even twist your own!

82/83 December eventide falls on the Ephrata Cloisters. In spartan surroundings, Seventh-Day German Baptists practiced vows of asceticism and celibacy from 1732 until 1934.

84 Hoofbeats will echo on the cold planks of a covered bridge and rubber tires will rumble through what some local folks romantically call a "Kissing Bridge."

85 It's a 45-minute round trip to Paradise aboard the Strasburg Railroad. Amish farmers are accustomed to coal-burning, smoke-belching locomotives chugging past their tobacco fields.

86 It's all in fun as the guilty party is unceremoniously dunked at Mt. Hope's rollicking recreation of a sixteenth-century Elizabethan Country Faire. Colorful events, including jousting and dueling, are held for 15 weekends starting in July.

87 Professional actors entertain at the Boar's Head Inn, part of the Renaissance Faire at Mt. Hope Estate and Winery, located just south of Exit 20 on the Pennsylvania Turnpike.

88/89 Lancaster's Penn Square is the focal point of a 90-minute walking tour. Heritage Center on the left dates from the 1790s. On the right is Watt and Shand Department Store. The local "skyscraper" in the center is the Griest Building.

CENTRAL PENNSYLVANIA

Central Pennsylvania is full of surprises. Certainly residents aren't modest about its virtues. On the Northern Tier, Potter County signs unabashedly declare it is "God's Country." Fully half the county is sparsely populated wilderness, a paradise for hunters. Spreading into Tioga County, the Endless Mountains provide such spectacular scenery that Pine Creek Gorge has been labeled the Grand Canyon of Pennsylvania. Rugged hills plunge a thousand feet down to a canyon that yields 50 miles of natural surprises. Enchanting Wellsboro serves as gateway to this mountain retreat. Beautifully planned with gas lights flickering on green islands, its boulevards are lined with gracious homes and well-tended lawns.

Scratch a Pennsylvanian and you'll find a sports fan. Little League baseball is major league in Williamsport, site of the World Series for junior athletes. When it comes to football, every Pennsylvanian is a rabid Penn State fan. What began in 1855 as Farmer's High School specializing in agriculture has expanded into a highly respected educational institution. In the splendor of the Nittany Mountains, Penn State University is every native's alma mater.

On the banks of the Susquehanna, Harrisburg, state capital since 1812, is dominated by the magnificent green glazed tile dome of its imposing capitol. Recently completed restoration and expansion of office space has resulted in a massive building of striking proportions and rich embellishment. The State Farm Show Complex hosts many events, but its Farm Show in January delights and educates thousands about Pennsylvania agriculture. Thirteen acres are enclosed to provide stabling and exhibit space for every conceivable animal and product of interest to the farm community.

Milton Snavely Hershey had only a fourth-grade education, but he possessed a good memory and persistence. In Denver, Colorado, he learned how to make caramels from fresh milk. That superior ingredient, plus the lessons of trial and error, led to his incredible success as a candy-maker. Hershey returned to Derry Township where he was born, good dairy country, and became a legend.

The tantalizing aroma of chocolate permeates the area, and Hershey Kiss streetlights adorn Chocolate Avenue. Hershey, planned by its founder, offers a regal hotel overlooking stunning gardens, an amusement park, museum, sports arena and stadium, tournament class golf courses and a free Chocolate World exhibit.

Hershey is more than just candy bars. M.S. and Catherine Hershey were childless. He liked to say that the Hershey Industrial School for orphan boys was "Kitty's idea." Today it is called Milton Hershey School. Twelve hundred boys and girls who have lost either parent receive a free home and tuition through high school.

The Battle of Gettysburg has been studied by military strategists from all over the world. One should stand quietly at The Angle and visualize Pickett's ill-fated charge across the open wheatfield. When the imaginary smoke of battle and memories of rows of white crosses have cleared, it's nice to remember that Dwight David Eisenhower chose to build the only permanent home he and Mamie ever enjoyed together in Gettysburg.

91 Freshly whitewashed fences surround lush blue-green meadows at Hanover Shoe Farms. Visitors are welcome to 4000 acres where trotters and pacers are bred to carry the name Hanover first across the finish line.

92/93 Like a Grant Wood painting, Adams County orchards create a formal pattern. Juicy red apples and golden ripe peaches are harvested in the area around Gettysburg.

94 The Pine Creek River flows through the gorge known as Pennsylvania's Grand Canyon in the Endless Mountains of Tioga County.

95 After the excitement of more than 30 thundering waterfalls and Kitchen Creek's three deep gorges, the sunlit lake at Rickett's Glen State Park offers quieter pleasures.

96 Not only Eve would be tempted by the perfection of these prime Adams County apples.

97 This smiling young contestant has worked long and hard to groom her snowy-white entry at the York Fair. One of the oldest fairs in the country, York Interstate Fair is typical of agricultural exhibits throughout the Commonwealth in autumn.

98 Every Little Leaguer dreams of playing in this stadium at the Little League World Series in Williamsport.

99 The Penn State Band accompanies wildly cheering partisans in the home section of Beaver Stadium. To many Pennsylvanians, Penn State means football.

100/101 Silent sentinels on Gettysburg battlefield, pieces of artillery remain as grim reminders of the bloodiest battle of the Civil War.

102 At its dedication in Harrisburg on
October 4, 1906, President Theodore
Roosevelt declared this to be "the hand-
somest state capitol in the nation." In classic
Italian Renaissance style, the exterior is
faced with granite from Vermont. The imposing 272-foot dome is covered with green
glazed tile.

103 Tulips enhance this view of the new East
Wing which links the North and South Office
Buildings of the state capitol and completes
the design conceived over 60 years ago.

104 This flamboyant beauty glistening in the sun is a 1941 Packard. In mid-October enthusiasts from the U.S. and Canada gather for the Antique Auto Show in Hershey, national headquarters for the Antique Automobile Club of America.

105 On a ridge commanding a view of Hershey and its manicured countryside stands Hotel Hershey, Pennsylvania's four star resort, noted for its gardens and variety of recreational opportunities.

106 "I would give everything I possess if I could call one of these boys my own." This statue in Founders Hall pays eloquent tribute to Milton and Catherine Hershey, founders of a school for orphans.

107 Santa gets into the spirit of Hershey's Christmas Candylane as bundled-up youngsters ride the carousel made by the renowned Philadelphia Toboggan Company.

108/109 Twilight magic settles on Hersheypark's Sky Ride and Giant Wheel.

WESTERN PENNSYLVANIA

The Erie Lowland in the northwest corner is a topographical contradiction to the rest of Pennsylvania. It is a virtually flat belt of land stretching along Lake Erie. A finger hooking into the lake, Presque Isle State Park's 12 sandy beaches lure vacationers to stroll through a wondrous variety of plants, or swim, bird-watch, fish, or just sunbathe in appreciation of the clear sparkling waters.

Erie, the state's only port on the Great Lakes, takes great pride in its center city. Restricted vehicular traffic permits one to explore the area on foot and to visit Erie's grand old library and the opulent Art Deco Warner Theater with its marvelous marquee. History buffs can relive the Battle of Lake Erie on the Brig Niagra commanded by Oliver Hazard Perry. The banner of his flagship admonished: "Don't Give Up the Ship." Nearby, a happy blend of soil and moderate weather allows vineyards to flourish. Wineries in neighboring North East produce some of the finest wines in the state.

Indians used the oil in Oil Creek externally as a medicine before enterprising settlers sold Seneca Oil as a lubricant and gentle laxative. By 1853, Dr. Francis Brewer of Titusville was skimming 18 gallons a day at a spring. Edwin Drake invested in the Pennsylvania Rock Oil Company (later Seneca Oil Company of Connecticut), searched for a borer, and the rest is fascinating history. For nearly 40 years after the successful drilling in 1859, Pennsylvania led the nation in oil production. The dramatic Pennsylvania oil saga is recaptured at Drake Well Memorial Park.

In 1753 George Washington recognized the potential of "the Land in the Fork" at the Ohio River because it had "absolute Command of both Rivers." A group of Virginians built Fort Prince George there only to relinquish it to the French, who dismantled it and properly fortified the point, calling it Fort Duquesne. After Braddock's disastrous attempt to capture Fort Duquesne, British troops under Colonel Henry Bouquet marched to the fort and discovered the French garrison had blown it up and retreated. General John Forbes renamed the site Fort Pitt and Colonel Bouquet was placed in command of the forks. Pittsburgh grew from this strategic position.

Its preeminence as the giant of manufacturing, the city of steel and iron, is legendary. The way Pittsburgh applied its muscle to changing its image and to cleansing its atmosphere is also applauded as one of the most dramatic reversals in this hemisphere. But the city is not resting on its laurels. As it approaches the twenty-first century, Renaissance II is in force, improving neighborhoods and attracting development in the old South Side around the dazzling restoration of Station Square. Renewal areas include the entire North Side as well as preservation and improvement of the riverfront on both sides of the Allegheny.

Now a booming corporate and financial center, Pittsburgh ranks as one of the top real estate markets in the country, according to U.S. News and World Report. Cultural excellence sets Pittsburgh apart with magnificent Heinz Hall, the serenely beautiful Scaife Art Gallery, and the world-famous Pittsburgh Symphony, as well as numerous libraries, universities, and colleges. No longer sluggish under a suffocating pall of grit and grime, Pittsburgh has a vitality that is infectious.

As the traveler approaches the Mason-Dixon line, he should seek out a special place, Fallingwater, the Kaufmann Conservation on Bear Run. A masterpiece of art as well as architecture, Frank Lloyd Wright's cantilevered design is a wonderful example of man and nature in harmony.

111 Pittsburgh is a city quite literally reborn. The Duquesne Incline affords a superb view of the Golden Triangle and Point Park Fountain as it leaps 150 feet into the air.

112/113 In the City of Bridges, Three Rivers Stadium is poised opposite the apex where the Allegheny and Monongahela merge to form the Ohio River.

114/115 Twilight works its sorcery on a city
that has shed its grime.

116 Although steelmaking is still Pittsburgh's
strength, mills like this one are gradually
being abandoned.

117 Row houses climb up a hill in Pittsburgh's
West End.

118 The striking tower of the giant Pittsburgh
Plate Glass Company polishes the skyline.

119 These fresh-faced modern buildings at
Fifth Avenue Place are proud statements of
Pittsburgh's rebirth.

120 The acclaimed Pittsburgh Symphony
presents its concert series in opulent Heinz
Hall.

121 Imposing medieval facades are on display at the Carnegie Institute of Technology.

123 Pittsburgh's popular Schenley Park provides pleasant surroundings for a bikers' rest stop.

124 Drake Well Museum near Titusville celebrates the world's first successful drilling for oil. This 85-foot derrick could bore down 2000 feet.

125 In 1936 Pittsburgh department store owner Edgar J. Kaufmann Jr. asked Frank Lloyd Wright to design a home overlooking the waterfalls on Bear Run. Fallingwater is the magnificent result.

126/127 White sails dot the blue waters of a mountain lake in Moraine State Park in Butler County.

122 Plunging along on frothy waters is exhilarating to white-water rafters on the Youghioheny River at Ohiopyle State Park.